# Making Sense of Everyday Idioms
# Horsing Around

BY KATHERINE SCRAPER

◆

GOOD YEAR BOOKS

Pearson Learning Group

The following people have contributed to the development of this product:

Art and Design: M. Jane Heelan, Liz Nemeth, Judy Mates

Editorial: Judy Adams, Tisha Hamilton

Manufacturing: Mark Cirillo, Thomas Dunne

Production: Karen Edmonds, Alia Lesser

Publishing Operations: Carolyn Coyle

Cover Illustration: Doug Roy

Interior Illustrations: George Hamblin

ISBN: 0-673-61735-1

Printed in the United States of America

1 2 3 4 5 6 7 8 9   06 05 04 03 02 01

This Book Is Printed
on Recycled Paper

1-800-321-3106
www.pearsonlearning.com

# Table of Contents

# Introduction

Idioms use words in a special way. We come to understand idioms best by reading or hearing them in contexts where they make sense. In *Horsing Around*, students have the opportunity to discover the intended meanings of 50 common idioms by seeing them used in many different and engaging contexts.

Knowledge of idioms is important for:

◆ oral language development

◆ reading comprehension

◆ creative writing

◆ practice for English Language Learners

Each reproducible sheet focuses on one idiom. That idiom is interpreted literally by a humorous illustration. After enjoying the illustration, students read a passage that contains the idiom and use the context of the passage to decipher the phrase. Then, on the lines below the passage, they explain what they think the idiom "really means."

Extend the basic activities by giving students the following challenges:

◆ Role-play the scenarios.

◆ On the reproducible cartoon frames, draw pictures and use speech balloons to demonstrate an understanding of an idiom's actual meaning.

◆ On the reproducible Story Sheet, use an idiom in a new written passage.

◆ Consult etymology books listed in the bibliography to research the origins of the expressions.

While your students are *horsing around*, you'll all be *shedding some light* on the English language. Enjoy!

# "Quit horsing around!"

"Please set the table while I finish making supper," Mr. Chung instructed Lin and Sam. Sam spread a tablecloth on the small dining table and got the knives, forks, spoons, and napkins. "You get the plates and glasses," he told Lin.

"Okay!" Lin replied as she skipped to the cupboard. She opened the door and reached for the dinnerware. Grinning, Lin balanced the plates on her head, and then began juggling the drinking glasses.

"Quit horsing around!" yelled Sam. "You'll break something!"

Sam really meant that _____

_____

_____

_____

_____

_____

_____

_____

# "It'll knock your socks off!"

Aunt Harriet was making chili. "I like it spicy. I'll add extra chili powder," she decided. Then she went out to the library.

Gloria came home. "M-m-m, chili!" she sighed. "I like it spicy. I'll add extra chili powder." Then she went into her room to start on her homework.

Allen came home. "Yum! Chili!" he said. Then he tasted a spoonful. His eyes widened, and he ran to the sink for a glass of water.

Just then there was a knock on the door. It was Allen's friend Donald. "Hey, Donald, do you want to stay for supper?" asked Allen. "We're having chili. It'll knock your socks off!"

◆ Allen really meant that _____

_____

_____

_____

_____

_____

# "It's time to bury the hatchet!"

"Thank you for taking care of my cat while I was away," said Mrs. Biddle. "Here are four free movie tickets to show my appreciation."

"Wow!" replied Amanda. "Thanks!"

Amanda rushed home to call her friends. "Hey, Kara, want to go to a movie this weekend? I have four free tickets!"

"Sure!" exclaimed Kara.

"Great. I'll call Zoe and Jennifer too," Amanda said.

"Don't ask Jennifer!" demanded Kara. "Remember when she made fun of my haircut? I haven't spoken to her since!"

"That was weeks ago, and she was only kidding," answered Amanda. "It's time to bury the hatchet!"

◆ Amanda really meant that _____

_____

_____

_____

_____

# "You really put your foot in your mouth!"

Sonny looked glum. "What's the matter?" asked his big brother, Sol.

"Today at school I was talking to my friends in the hall," explained Sonny. "I told them I like every class except math. They all got funny looks on their faces. When I turned around I saw Mr. Holly, my math teacher, standing right behind me!"

"You really put your foot in your mouth!" exclaimed Sol.

◆ Sol really meant that _____

_____

_____

_____

_____

_____

_____

_____

# "Don't let the cat out of the bag!"

"Mr. DeMarco is reading the best book to us in class!" Joelle commented at supper one night. "It's about a boy who gets a job at a nature center. He gets to help take care of an eagle with a broken wing. The eagle doesn't like anyone but him. Then one day the eagle gets sick, and the boy tries to raise money to buy medicine for the sick bird. The boy has to give a big speech in front of the city council. Oh, and he's having all kinds of problems at home with his parents. And his friends are mad because he doesn't spend time with them anymore, and . . ."

"Hey, I read that book," said Joelle's brother, Max. "It was a good one. In the end . . ."

"Stop!" interrupted Joelle. "Don't let the cat out of the bag!"

◆ Joelle really meant that _____

_____

_____

_____

_____

# "It's straight from the horse's mouth!"

"Thanks for calling, Uncle Harry!" Tyson said happily. He hung up the phone and immediately dialed the number of his best friend, Kyle. "Hey, Kyle, want to go sledding in the morning?"

"But . . ." began Kyle.

"And then we can make a snowman, and build a snow fort and have a snowball fight. And then maybe my big sister will make us some cookies and hot chocolate and we can play video games all afternoon, and . . ."

"Slow down!" exclaimed Kyle. "Tomorrow's a school day, remember?"

"No, it's not, it's a SNOW day!" Tyson replied. "You know my uncle's the principal, right? Well, he just called to give me the news. It's straight from the horse's mouth!"

◆ Tyson really meant that _____

_____

_____

_____

_____

# "She's a penny pincher!"

Patty knocked on the Peterson's door. Mr. Peterson answered. "The school band is selling carnations to raise money for a trip to Band Day," said Patty politely. "The flowers are fifty cents each."

"I'll take one!" decided Mr. Peterson.

"Thank you!" said Patty. She'd sold almost 30 carnations! Then Patty spied the house across the street. Everyone in the neighborhood called it "The Radclif Mansion."

Mrs. Radclif was home. Patty told her about the flowers, sure of another sale, but Mrs. Radclif replied, "Fifty cents just for a carnation? I'll not be buying any!" Then she firmly closed the door.

"Wow!" Patty thought as she walked away. I'm never trying to sell anything to Mrs. Radclif again. She's a penny pincher!"

◆ Patty really meant that _____

_____

_____

_____

_____

_____

# "He drives me up the wall!"

"So how's that new boy, Phil, doing?" asked Brent at breakfast one morning.

"How did you know about Phil?" Courtney sputtered.

"The same way I know about your fight with Ramona, the D+ you got on your math test, and the CD player you're hoping for," Brent replied with a grin.

"You've been reading my diary again!" shouted Courtney. "It's private! You shouldn't be snooping in it!"

"Better find a new hiding place," Brent taunted as he left for school. "Bye, bye, kiddo!"

Courtney stomped into her room muttering, "Why do I have to have a brother? He drives me up the wall!"

◆ Courtney really meant that _____

_____

_____

_____

_____

# "Come on, shake a leg!"

Mrs. Kelso pushed back her plate and wiped her mouth with the napkin.

"I'd like the two of you to wash the dishes," she said to Katey and Robin. "I have a lot of reading to do for my class tomorrow."

"Okay, Mom," agreed Robin.

"I have a quick phone call to make first," said Katey. "Go ahead and start without me."

Robin ran soapy water into the sink, and carried in all the dirty dishes. She put the leftovers in the refrigerator, shook out the tablecloth, and pushed in the chairs. Katey was still on the phone.

"Come on, shake a leg!" Robin hollered. "We're supposed to be doing this together!"

◆ Robin really meant that

# "What have you got up your sleeve?"

"Get out!" Danny called to his sister, Sara. "I'm trying to read, and you're hanging out in my room again! I'm tired of you getting into my stuff!"

"I just wanted to ask if you'd like some popcorn," replied Sara sweetly. "I was getting ready to make some and thought I'd share it with you."

Danny hesitated. "Sure I'd like some," he admitted. Sara left and soon returned with a large bowl of popcorn and some lemonade.

"Here you go," she began. "Now, would you like me to start your laundry for you? I've got plenty of time!"

Danny looked up from his book, wrinkling his forehead. "You're never this nice to me," he said suspiciously. "What have you got up your sleeve?"

◆ Danny really meant that _____

_____

_____

_____

_____

# "That's a real feather in your cap!"

Tia's sister Tanya came running into her room, waving the newspaper. "Look, Tia!" she exclaimed. "You made the front page!"

Tia saw the headline, "Local Girl Saves a Life." Then she read on, "Tia McKinney, age 12, was eating dinner in an area restaurant when a man at a nearby table began to choke on a piece of steak. Tia quickly applied the Heimlich Maneuver, which she had learned in health class. The steak dislodged, but Tia called 911 just to be sure the man was OK. The grateful man is doing fine and Tia will be given a Community Hero award at the next City Council meeting."

"I'm so proud of you," Tanya said as she hugged Tia. "Not many people earn the Community Hero award. That's a real feather in your cap!"

Tanya really meant that _____

_____

_____

_____

_____

# "Don't spill the beans!"

Dad's birthday was the next day, and Mitsu and Josh had no money to buy him a gift. "I know," exclaimed Josh at breakfast. "We could clean out the shed!"

"Good idea," agreed Mitsu. "Let's start right after school."

At 3:00, Josh and Mitsu hurried home. They pulled out the lawnmower, toolbox, trash cans, bicycles, sports equipment, and gardening tools. They dusted off the shelves and swept the floor. They hammered nails into the wall and hung up the small items. Then they put everything back neatly, and closed the shed door.

"Remember, it's a surprise," cautioned Mitsu. "Don't spill the beans!"

◆ Mitsu really meant that _____

_____

_____

_____

_____

_____

NAME

# "I have butterflies in my stomach!"

"Q-U-I-C-K-L-Y," spelled Keisha.

"Right," said David. "Now you give me one."

"INTRODUCTION," said Keisha.

"I-N-T-R-O-D-U-C-T-I-O-N," David slowly spelled out. "That was an easy one."

"Good job! Let's stop now. We've been practicing for weeks for the spelling bee. Tomorrow, it'll all be over and I'll bet we win," Keisha assured David.

"I know, I know!" groaned David. "We're the best spellers in our class. We hardly ever miss a word. We've gone over and over the extra lists the teacher gave us. But I can't help it . . . I have butterflies in my stomach!"

◆ David really meant that _____

_____

_____

_____

_____

_____

_____

# "Has the cat got your tongue?"

Emma trudged home from school. It was her birthday, and no one in her family had remembered. Her friends at school hadn't said a word about it, either. Ms. Clark, Emma's favorite teacher, had forgotten, too. Instead, she had asked Emma to stay after school to help set up for the science fair.

Emma opened the front door of her apartment, and suddenly heard a loud, "SURPRISE!" She looked around. There were balloons, presents, and a huge cake on the table. Dad, Aunt Rita, Emma's sister, Shelly, Ms. Clark, and all Emma's friends were there. Emma just stood there, staring and grinning.

"What's the matter, Emma?" teased Shelly. "Has the cat got your tongue?"

◆ Shelly really meant that _____

_____

_____

_____

_____

# "He left me high and dry!"

"Your science projects are due Friday," Mrs. Judd reminded her class. "Partners must present their results on a poster. It will count toward your total grade, so do your best!"

Mario caught up with Gary in the hall. "You've missed every meeting we've set up so far," he said. "We only have a few more days."

"Sorry, Mario. I've been really busy with basketball. How about Thursday? I'll come over right after practice," Gary told him.

Late Thursday night, Mario's mother knocked on his bedroom door. "It's time for bed. What are you working on, honey?" she asked.

"I'm finishing the science poster Gary and I were supposed to make together," Mario sighed. "He left me high and dry!"

◆ Mario really meant that _____

_____

_____

_____

_____

# "You're on the right track!"

"Let's look at story problem nine," Ms. Singh said. "There are 19 students in a class. They write in their journals each day. On Tuesday, two students were absent. On Thursday, four students were absent. On Friday, one student was absent. How many journal entries did the class make that week?"

Clay raised his hand. "Yes, Clay?" called Ms. Singh.

"First you multiply 19 times 5, because there are five days of school in a week. Then you have to subtract when the kids were gone, because they couldn't write in their journals those days. So that would be. . . . let's see. . . ." Clay hesitated.

"Keep going, Clay!" encouraged Ms. Singh. "You're on the right track!"

◆ Ms. Singh really meant that _____

_____

_____

_____

_____

_____

NAME

# "I'd better hit the road!"

It was raining hard. As Ricky hurried home from school, he spotted Mrs. Gray trying to carry two bags of groceries in from her car. "Let me help," Ricky called, taking a bag from Mrs. Gray and running ahead to open the heavy door of her apartment building.

"Thank you!" exclaimed Mrs. Gray, putting down her bag and shaking the water from her hair. "Do you have time for some cookies?"

"Sorry, but my dad is expecting me," replied Ricky. "I'd better hit the road!"

◆ Ricky really meant that _____

# "That's a fly in the ointment!"

Bree slammed her locker shut, adjusted her backpack on her shoulder, and turned to her waiting friend.

"Did you ask Mary to study with us tonight?" she asked Kim.

Kim shrugged. "Yesterday I did. We had it all worked out that my cousin would drive the three of us to the library right after supper. Mary was going to bring a book she found to help with our report. She even had new colored pencils to use on the map we're making. But then today she remembered she had to work in the refreshment stand at the volleyball game at the same time."

"That's a fly in the ointment!" Bree moaned.

◆ Bree really meant that _____

_____

_____

_____

_____

_____

# "Keep it under your hat!"

"Hi, Allison!" Molly said as she walked into her friend's room. "WOW! Where did you get all that money?"

Allison counted, "Twenty-one, twenty-two, twenty-three. . . I have twenty-three dollars and nineteen cents. I've been saving my allowance, and Mom gave me money for playing with the baby while she studied, and Grandma sent me ten dollars for my birthday," Allison replied.

"What are you going to do with it?" Molly asked.

"I don't know yet," Allison confessed. "But I do know that if my big brother finds out that I have money, he'll want to borrow some. So keep it under your hat!"

◆ **Allison really meant that** _____

_____

_____

_____

_____

_____

# "I'm sitting pretty now!"

Jill had been anxiously awaiting the day when her big sister Lucy would leave for college so she could have the bedroom they shared all to herself. Just think! She could listen to the music she liked, decorate the room any way she wanted, and have her own dresser and closet.

The day arrived for Lucy to go. After waving to her sister from the driveway, Jill dashed upstairs and began re-arranging the furniture and hanging some new posters on the walls. Finally, she was done.

Just then, Jill's father looked in. "How do you like having your own room?" he asked.

"I'm sitting pretty now!" Jill replied happily.

◆ Jill really meant that _____

_____

_____

_____

_____

_____

# "He's the big cheese around here!"

Caleb liked to go to the park after school and on weekends to play basketball with other kids in the neighborhood. It was especially fun when Todd was there. Todd was the smallest boy on the court, but he could out-dribble and out-shoot anyone.

One Saturday, a new boy named Wesley came, just as the boys were picking teams. "We want Todd!" shouted one group.

"You had Todd on your team last time! We get Todd," insisted the other group.

"Why does everyone want the short guy?" Wesley asked Caleb.

"He may be little, but he's the big cheese around here!" Caleb replied.

◆ Caleb really meant that _____

_____

_____

_____

_____

_____

_____

# "Let him off the hook!"

Jeff's mother answered the phone.

"Hello, Mrs. Rich? This is Ms. Mendosa, Jeff's math teacher. I wanted to discuss Jeff's grades with you."

"Ms. Mendosa," said Jeff's mother, "after that last report card we've been making Jeff do extra math homework every night. We don't allow him to use the phone or watch TV, and he has to recite his multiplication tables before he goes to bed. I just don't know what more we can do!"

Ms. Mendosa laughed. "That's not why I'm calling," she replied. "I wanted you to know that he got the top score on the last test and he now has an A. I think you can let him off the hook!"

◆ Ms. Mendosa really meant that _____

_____

_____

_____

_____

NAME _____

# "You'll bring down the house!"

"Have you seen Ellen?" Ms. Bernini asked frantically. "The play starts in ten minutes!"

"She has on her costume and makeup," replied Asa. "But I don't know where she is."

Ms. Bernini looked for Ellen backstage, then tried the prop room. There she found Ellen sitting on the floor with her head down.

"What are you doing?" Ms. Bernini began. "Why, Ellen, you've been crying!"

"I'm scared!" Ellen confessed. "I'm afraid I'll forget my lines. I don't want to disappoint the Drama Club."

"You've worked hard," Ms. Bernini encouraged Ellen. "And you're a natural. Come on out and give it your best try. You'll bring down the house!"

◆ Ms. Bernini really meant that _____

_____

_____

_____

_____

_____

NAME _____

# "He's sure hot under the collar!"

Ross, Levi, and Matt were studying together for a math test. Ross was explaining how to do a problem.

"Oh, I get it!" Levi interrupted. He punched some numbers into the calculator. "See? Ross, that's the same answer you came up with. That's the fifth time you and I got the same answer!"

"This is stupid," Matt shouted, throwing down his math book. "You two think you're so smart. I'm not wasting my time here." Matt stomped out of the room, slamming the door behind him.

"I wonder what's bothering him," said Ross, shaking his head.

"Yeah, he's sure hot under the collar!" exclaimed Levi.

◆ Levi really meant that _____

_____

_____

_____

_____

# "You're pulling my leg!"

Hector and Andy looked at the floor of their bedroom. It was littered with clothes, shoes, books, papers, snack wrappers, and sports equipment. "I want this all picked up before you go to the softball game," declared their father.

Hector groaned but Andy waited until their father was out of sight, then whispered, "He said to pick it up. He didn't say to put it away! Let's throw it all in the closet!" The boys got busy, and five minutes later they shouted, "Papa, we're finished!"

"You're pulling my leg!" their father called back.

◆ The boys' father really meant that _____

_____

_____

_____

_____

_____

_____

# "She's a bookworm!"

"I got a new board game. Want to come over and try it out?" Julie asked her friend Maya on the phone.

"Sure!" said Maya. "How many people can play?"

"It takes four," replied Julie. "My brother said he'd play with us."

"I'd bring my sister, but I don't think I can get her to stop reading, even for a new game. She's a bookworm!" explained Maya.

Maya really meant that _____

_____

_____

_____

_____

_____

_____

# "Don't throw in the towel!"

Lindsey was making cookies when the phone rang. It was her best friend. Lindsey walked around the kitchen with the phone tucked under her chin, measuring and mixing as she chatted. She didn't notice that she used salt instead of sugar.

An hour later, Lindsey was taking the cookies out of the oven just as her brother Rob came in. "Have a cookie!" she offered.

"Thanks!" agreed Rob, stuffing the whole cookie into his mouth. Suddenly his eyes widened. "Ugh! It's awful!" He rushed to the sink for a glass of water.

Lindsey looked as if she were going to cry. "I'm never going to make cookies again!" she declared.

"Don't throw in the towel!" Rob retorted. "Just try following the recipe next time!"

◆ Rob really meant that _____

_____

_____

_____

_____

_____

# "She blew her top!"

"Hank Wolf, what are you doing?" called Dr. Wolf, as Hank ran past her up the stairs without a word. Hank slammed his bedroom door. "I'd better go check this out," decided Hank's mother.

"Hank!" shouted Dr. Wolf, as she knocked on the door.

"Come in," mumbled Hank.

Hank's mother went in and saw Hank sitting on the side of his bed staring at the floor. "What's wrong, son?" asked Dr. Wolf.

"You'll probably be getting a phone call from Mrs. Anson next door," Hank began. "I was practicing hitting my new baseball in the lot out back. I hit a long one, and it broke Mrs. Anson's patio door. She blew her top!"

◆ Hank really meant that _____

_____

_____

_____

_____

_____

# "She's on cloud nine!"

All Latonia ever talked about was horses. She read horse books, watched horse movies, collected toy horses, drew horses, and even dreamed about horses.

One day, Latonia got a letter from her grandmother. "When I was your age," Latonia read, "I wanted a horse more than anything. But I lived in the city just as you do, and I never even got to pet one. I recently read about a summer camp for families. There are trail rides every afternoon. Would you like to go with me? We could learn to ride together. Ask your parents to give me a call! Love, Grandma."

Latonia's father called her grandmother that evening. "Sure, Latonia can go to camp with you," he replied. "She's on cloud nine!"

◆ Latonia's father really meant that _____

_____

_____

_____

_____

# "Are you down in the dumps?"

"Hey, Eli, do you want to shoot some hoops?" Josiah asked.

"Nah," replied Eli.

"Well, do you want to help me work on my bike? You fixed yours, so maybe you could give me some ideas," Josiah said.

"Not today," said Eli glumly.

"I need to drop some books by the library. Do you want to go along? We could stop for ice cream on the way home!" Josiah suggested.

"No, thanks," Eli sighed.

"What's the matter, are you down in the dumps?" asked Josiah.

◆ Josiah really meant that _____

_____

_____

_____

_____

_____

_____

NAME _____

# "You hit the nail on the head!"

Brittany had just moved to a new school, and she was nervous about her classes. Since social studies was her hardest subject, she decided to take her book home every night to study ahead.

One day her teacher, Mr. Sanchez, announced, "We're starting a new unit on inventors. Does anyone know who invented dozens of uses for peanuts?" Brittany looked around. Everyone in the class seemed puzzled, so she slowly raised her hand.

"Yes, Brittany?" Mr. Sanchez called.

"It's George Washington Carver," she answered.

"You hit the nail on the head!" Mr. Sanchez exclaimed.

◆ Mr. Sanchez really meant that _____

_____

_____

_____

_____

_____

# "Get your head out of the clouds!"

"Coach Cooper finally let me play goalie!" exclaimed Pete as he ran to his position. "Come on, bring the ball to me," he yelled. "See what I do with it!"

Pete watched the action at the other end of the field. "I wonder what it would be like playing professional soccer," thought Pete. "No one would ever score on me! I'd be the most famous goalie ever! I'd be rich! Everywhere I went kids would want my autograph! Teams would fight over who got me! Everyone would say . . ."

WHIZ! Suddenly the ball flew over Pete's shoulder. Everyone on the team groaned loudly. "Pete, get your head out of the clouds!" yelled Coach Cooper.

◆ Coach Cooper really meant that _____

_____

_____

_____

_____

_____

# "That's a pretty kettle of fish!"

The science fair was only a day away! Vanessa raided her mother's rag bag for scraps of brightly-colored fabric. Using a needle and thread, she carefully hand-stitched a mini parachute.

Finally Vanessa's parachute was ready, and she decided to test it in the backyard. Then it happened. The neighbor's cat grabbed the parachute in mid-flight, shredding it with its sharp claws. Vanessa tried to get it back, but that only made things worse. Now all Vanessa had left was a tangled ball of torn fabric and thread. "What will I tell my teacher?" Vanessa cried.

The next morning, Vanessa explained to her teacher, Mrs. Phan, what had happened to her last-minute project. "That's a pretty kettle of fish!" Mrs. Phan exclaimed.

◆ Mrs. Phan really meant that _____

_____

_____

_____

_____

# "She got cold feet!"

"Me? Go to the principal's office?" sputtered Saleena. "Why me?"

"Because you're our student council representative, and it's your job to ask the principal if we can have a class carnival to raise money for our field trip," Ms. Redding explained.

Everyone stared at Saleena. "Okay," she sighed. "I'll go. But I've never been to the principal's office before."

Saleena was back in three minutes. "What did the principal say?" the students asked. Saleena just looked at the floor.

"I'll bet she got cold feet!" muttered Vance.

◆ Vance really meant that _____

_____

_____

_____

_____

_____

# "It's raining cats and dogs!"

Field Day was coming up, and all the students were practicing. Jake was throwing a football, and Greta was running the 100-yard dash. Scott, Matthew, and Richie were in the three-legged race, and Nina was in the free-throw contest. Altogether there were twelve events.

The big day finally arrived. Dark clouds covered the sky as the students met in the schoolyard. The principal, Mr. Choi, blew his whistle. "It's time for the races. Line up by class!" he called.

Just then, large raindrops began to fall, slowly at first, then faster and harder. Mr. Choi blew his whistle again. "Everyone back inside!" he announced.

"It's raining cats and dogs! No Field Day today," Nina shouted as she ran indoors.

Nina really meant that _____
_____
_____
_____
_____

# "We're all in the same boat!"

"I can barely lift my backpack," complained Quincy. "I have to study for a math test. My report about the Constitution needs to be typed tonight. We have a concert coming up, so I have to drag my trumpet home. I have to answer all the unit questions for science, and I have nine more chapters to read for my book report. And the worst part is that my favorite TV show is on tonight and I won't even have time to watch it!"

Aaron and Sherry frowned. "Look at our backpacks, Quincy," demanded Aaron. "We go to this school, too, and have the same teachers you do. We're all in the same boat!"

◆ Aaron really meant that _____

_____

_____

_____

_____

_____

_____

# "Wake up and smell the coffee!"

Daria just couldn't stop thinking about the camping trip coming up. Her dad was going to pick her up right after school and they would go to the grocery store to buy some food and supplies. Daria's father had a new tent and sleeping bags. The two of them would build a campfire and tell stories, then get up early to go fishing. They would hike in the woods, hunt for fossils, and . . .

"Daria? What is the answer?" demanded Mr. Morgan.

"Uh . . . George Washington?" guessed Daria.

"Wake up and smell the coffee, Daria!" whispered My Ling. "This is math class!"

◆ My Ling really meant that _____

_____

_____

_____

_____

_____

_____

# "He got up on the wrong side of the bed!"

"Pass it! Pass it!" yelled Lionel. He and his friend Brad were watching football on TV. Another friend, Cory, knocked on the door.

"Hey, Cory!" greeted Lionel. "Come watch the game with us! It's your favorite team!"

"Aw, I wanted you guys to go to the park with me," Cory pouted, spinning a soccer ball between his fingers.

"Sure, as soon as the game's over," Brad replied. "Want some popcorn?"

"You guys never do what I want to do," Cory exclaimed. "I'm leaving."

Lionel and Brad watched Cory stomp away. "I've never seen Cory act like that," Lionel observed. "I'd say he got up on the wrong side of the bed!"

◆ Lionel really meant that _____

_____

_____

_____

_____

# "You have a frog in your throat!"

Lydia couldn't wait for the class musical. She had the lead, and had been practicing for weeks. The night before the opening, she went to rehearsal early to practice with the pianist. Lydia stayed afterward to go over her solos with Mrs. Nolan one last time.

Later that evening, Lydia went into her mother's study with tears in her eyes. "What's wrong, Lydia?" her mother asked.

"I can't talk right," Lydia squeaked. "What if I miss the show?"

"You've been singing more than usual, so now you have a frog in your throat," Lydia's mother told her. "All you need is a good night's sleep."

◆ Lydia's mother really meant that _____

_____

_____

_____

_____

_____

_____

# "You're barking up the wrong tree!"

"Joel, I have a favor to ask," Cammie began. "I need to borrow ten dollars. Mom said I could go to the concert with Hannah if I could earn the money. Usually I babysit for the Yoo's every weekend, but their kids have been sick so they haven't called. And I had to pay a fine at the library for that book I thought I lost, and I had to buy a birthday present for Ny's party. You're the best brother in the world and I knew I could count . . ."

"Whoa! Slow down, Cammie," Joel replied. "I already spent my allowance this week. You're barking up the wrong tree!"

◆ Joel really meant that _____

_____

_____

_____

_____

_____

_____

# "Put your money where your mouth is!"

Charlie clicked off his stopwatch and put his hands on his knees, breathing hard. Then he wiped his forehead and took a long drink from his water bottle.

"I can't wait until the school track meet!" exclaimed Charlie. "I've been running a mile every day after school. I'll bet I'm the fastest runner in our class!"

"Angela is pretty speedy," commented Seth. "She beat everyone last year. And she practices just as much as you do."

"But she's a girl," explained Charlie. "I'll be way ahead of her."

Just then, Angela walked up. "I heard that, Charlie," she said. "Put your money where your mouth is. Let's race right now!"

◆ Angela really meant that _____

_____

_____

_____

_____

# "He plays by ear!"

"It was nice of Rodney to play the piano for the pancake supper," commented Mrs. Gardner. "He's very talented! It made the meal all the more enjoyable."

"Oh, I'll bet he was just trying to get out of washing dishes," teased Gus. "All the other scouts had to take a turn in the kitchen."

"Well, both jobs were important, and your troop made quite a bit of money to help pay for camp," replied Mrs. Gardner. "By the way, how long has Rodney taken piano lessons?"

"He's never had a lesson in his life," explained Gus. "He plays by ear!"

◆ Gus really meant that _____

_____

_____

_____

_____

_____

_____

_____

# "She really got my goat!"

Juan jumped as a rock hit his tree house. "What was that?" he asked Greg.

"It's Susie!" exclaimed Greg as he peered over the edge. "What do you want, Susie?" he called.

"Do you boys want to come see my new clubhouse?" Susie inquired sweetly. "My uncle built it for me in my backyard. It has two rooms and real windows and a door that locks. And no boys are allowed inside!"

"Go away!" Juan yelled. Susie giggled and walked back home. "She just did that because we wouldn't let her and her friends play in the treehouse," Juan pouted. "Susie is trouble. She really got my goat!"

◆ Juan really meant that _____

_____

_____

_____

_____

_____

_____

# "Maybe that will shed some light on it!"

"Come on, you can do it this time!" Anna whispered in Smokey's ear. She sat up straight, and got a firm hold on the reins. She nudged her heels into Smokey's sides, and called "Giddyup!"

Smokey walked, then trotted, and then cantered, responding to Anna's voice and the pressure of her knees. "Okay, here we go!" Anna instructed as they came to a practice fence.

Smokey suddenly swung around and stopped, refusing to jump. "Not again!" Anna sighed.

Mrs. Barkley, her trainer, ran over. "Good try, Anna," she said. "Why don't you watch this time as I jump my horse? Listen to how I use my voice when I give the command to jump. Maybe that will shed some light on it!"

◆ Mrs. Barkley really meant that _____

_____

_____

_____

_____

# "He has a chip on his shoulder!"

Gina walked to the end of the diving board, jumped as high as she could, and curled into a little ball. She was just straightening out her body when she crashed into the water, back first. "Ow!" groaned Gina, as she climbed out of the pool. "I didn't quite make it all the way around. That hurt!"

Becky grinned. "Yeah I bet! Russell here did a belly-buster the other day, and I thought I'd have to call 911!"

"Look who's talking," Russell retorted. "You're not exactly an Olympic champion yourself!" Then he turned and strode away.

"I guess I shouldn't kid Russell," sighed Becky. "Sometimes he has a chip on his shoulder."

◆ Becky really meant that _____

_____

_____

_____

_____

_____

# "I'll try to butter her up!"

"What's the matter?" asked Cherise. "You look really upset!"

"I am," replied Tommy. "I have a D in band! My mom will ground me for life!"

"How did you get a D?" asked Cherise.

"We're supposed to practice 15 minutes every night, and get our practice card signed. I keep forgetting to take my saxophone home. Mrs. Carson said the only way I can catch up and raise my grade before report cards come out is to practice an hour every day, even on weekends!" explained Tommy.

"Maybe you should give up TV for a while!" suggested Cherise.

"No way!" exclaimed Tommy. "I'm going to go see Mrs. Carson again. I'll try to butter her up!"

◆ Tommy really meant that _____

_____

_____

_____

_____

# "He's all thumbs!"

Mikel was talking on the phone when he heard a crash in the next room. "Hold on, I'll be right back!" he said.

His brother, Alex, was picking up pieces of plastic from the floor. Some of them were glued together at odd angles, and others looked broken. Squashed-up tubes and sticky paintbrushes were lying on the newspaper-covered table. Spots of color shone on Alex's face.

"Is that your model airplane?" Mikel asked.

"Yeah," muttered Alex. "This is harder than I thought it would be."

Mikel rushed back to the phone. "I'll call you later," he promised. "I need to go help my little brother with a project. He's all thumbs!"

◆ Mikel really meant that _____

_____

_____

_____

_____

# "I'll try to pull some strings!"

"Wow! Where did you get that card?" asked Alejandro. "I've been looking all over for one!"

"I bought it at my uncle's new card shop," replied Jackson.

"Where is your uncle's place?" asked Alejandro.

"It's downtown, just inside the mall," explained Jackson. "Saturday he's having a grand opening. The first hour is by invitation only, and he's getting some professional players to come in and sign their cards."

"I'd give anything if I could go!" sighed Alejandro.

"Maybe you can," remarked Jackson. "I'll try to pull some strings!"

Jackson really meant that _____

_____

_____

_____

_____

# "It's on the house!"

Tina walked up and down the aisles at the department store looking for poster board for her art project. She finally found some among the office supplies. As she reached for it, she spotted a broken bottle of ink that had spilled all over the packages of envelopes.

Just then, the manager walked by. "Ma'am," Tina said politely. "There's a broken jar on this shelf. Someone might get covered with ink, or cut themselves. I thought you'd want to know."

"Why, thank you," replied the manager. "I'll get that cleaned up right away. How thoughtful you are! Here, let me carry your poster board out for you. You can put your wallet away. It's on the house!"

◆ The manager really meant that _____

_____

_____

_____

_____

_____

# "She stole the spotlight!"

Naomi was glad to see her mother, up and feeling better when she got home. "We missed you at the concert," Naomi told her.

"Naomi's hard work really paid off," her father added. "She did a great job tonight."

"I can't wait until my next piano recital! I think I'll start practicing an extra hour every day," Naomi chattered excitedly.

"Take it easy," her mother said, laughing. "Your father just said you played very well."

"She played better than very well," Naomi's father said. "I didn't think the audience would ever stop clapping."

"A lot of parents came up to me afterwards," Naomi said. "One lady told me I stole the spotlight!"

◆ The lady really meant that _____

_____

_____

_____

_____

Making Sense of Everyday Idioms: Horsing Around

# CARTOON FRAMES

# Story Sheet

◆ Idiom: _____

◆ My Story: _____

_____

_____

_____

_____

_____

_____

_____

_____

_____

_____

_____

_____

_____

_____

# Answer Key

*"Quit horsing around!"* Sam really meant that Lin should stop being wild and silly.

*"It'll knock your socks off!"* Allen really meant that Donald would be surprised when he tasted Aunt Harriet's chili; it was amazingly spicy!

*"It's time to bury the hatchet!"* Amanda really meant that Kara should forgive Jennifer and resume their friendship.

*"You really put your foot in your mouth!"* Sol really meant that Sonny had said the wrong thing at the wrong time and probably offended his math teacher.

*"Don't let the cat out of the bag!"* Joelle really meant that she didn't want Max to reveal how the story ended; she wanted it to be a surprise.

*"It's straight from the horse's mouth!"* Tyson really meant that he had heard the news from the person who was most qualified to give it; he was not just guessing or hoping.

*"She's a penny pincher!"* Patty really meant that Mrs. Radclif wasn't willing to spend any of her money, even for an inexpensive item or for a good cause.

*"He drives me up the wall!"* Courtney really meant that she was very annoyed with Brent; he always did things to make her angry.

*"Come on, shake a leg!"* Robin really meant that she wanted Katey to hurry up.

*"What have you got up your sleeve?"* Danny really meant that he was afraid Sara was only being nice to him for a reason she was keeping secret.

*"That's a real feather in your cap!"* Tanya really meant that Tia had received a well-deserved honor.

*"Don't spill the beans!"* Mitsu really meant that she didn't want Josh to reveal their secret to their father.

*"I have butterflies in my stomach!"* David really meant that he was very nervous about doing well in the spelling bee.

*"Has the cat got your tongue?"* Shelly really meant that maybe Emma was so surprised she couldn't talk.

*"He left me high and dry!"* Mario really meant that Gary had deserted him; he never showed up to fulfill his responsibilities.

*"You're on the right track!"* Ms. Singh really meant that Clay had a good start in figuring out the answer; he was using the correct process, and needed to keep working until he got it.

*"I'd better hit the road!"* Ricky really meant that he needed to leave right away.

*"That's a fly in the ointment!"* Bree really meant that one problem was spoiling the plans the girls made.

*"Keep it under your hat!"* Allison really meant that she didn't want Molly to tell anyone about the money Allison had saved.

*"I'm sitting pretty now!"* Jill really meant that having her own room was a luxury that made her happy.

*"He's the big cheese around here!"* Caleb really meant that Todd was a leader and was considered the most important player in the group.

*"Let him off the hook!"* Ms. Mendosa really meant that Mrs. Rich should return things to their original state and give Jeff back his privileges.

*"You'll bring down the house!"* Ms. Bernini really meant that the crowd would cheer loudly at Ellen's performance; everyone would be impressed with her acting abilities.

*"He's sure hot under the collar!"* Levi really meant that Matt's behavior and words indicated that he was very angry about something.

*"You're pulling my leg!"* The boys' father really meant that the boys were trying to fool him, and that they couldn't have finished cleaning their room so quickly.

*"She's a bookworm!"* Maya really meant that her sister loved reading more than anything.

*"Don't throw in the towel!"* Rob really meant that Lindsey shouldn't give up just because of one failure.

*"She blew her top!"* Hank really meant that Mrs. Anson had reacted very angrily toward him.

*"She's on cloud nine!"* Latonia's father really meant that Latonia was very happy; her dream had come true!

*"Are you down in the dumps?"* Josiah really meant that Eli seemed to be feeling bad or sad about something.

*"You hit the nail on the head!"* Mr. Sanchez really meant that Brittany had given exactly the right answer.

*"Get your head out of the clouds!"* Coach Cooper really meant that Pete should stop daydreaming and pay attention.

*"That's a pretty kettle of fish!"* Mrs. Phan really meant that unusual events had caused quite a problem.

*"She got cold feet!"* Vance really meant that Saleena had been too afraid to talk to the principal.

*"It's raining cats and dogs!"* Nina really meant that it was raining very hard outside.

*"We're all in the same boat!"* Aaron really meant that Quincy should quit complaining because he and Sherry had a lot of work to do, too.

*"Wake up and smell the coffee!"* My Ling really meant that Daria needed to pay attention to what was going on around her.

*"He got up on the wrong side of the bed!"* Lionel really meant that Cory was being grouchy for no reason.

*"You have a frog in your throat!"* Lydia's mother really meant that Lydia's voice was hoarse.

*"You're barking up the wrong tree!"* Joel really meant that Cammie was asking the wrong person; he was not in a position to help her.

*"Put your money where your mouth is!"* Angela really meant that she was challenging Charlie to show whether or not he could really beat her in a race.

*"He plays by ear!"* Gus really meant that Rodney could listen to a song, then reproduce the tune on the piano without being able to read music.

*"She really got my goat!"* Juan really meant that Susie's behavior had annoyed him; Susie had made him angry.

*"Maybe that will shed some light on it!"* Mrs. Barkley really meant that by watching her make her horse jump, Anna might get a better idea of how to teach her horse to jump.

*"He has a chip on his shoulder!"* Becky really meant that Russell sometimes thought people were being mean to him when they really weren't.

*"I'll try to butter her up!"* Tommy really meant that he was going to compliment Mrs. Carson and act so nice to her that she would not make Tommy work for a good grade.

*"He's all thumbs!"* Mikel really meant that Alex had difficulty making things with his hands.

*"I'll try to pull some strings!"* Jackson really meant that he would ask his uncle to do him a favor and let him bring Alejandro to the card-signing.

*"It's on the house!"* The manager really meant that she would give Tina the poster board for free to show her appreciation for Tina's help.

*"She stole the spotlight!"* The lady really meant that Naomi had played the piano very well and she was the star of the evening.

# Bibliography

Ammer, Christine. *The American Heritage Dictionary of Idioms.* Houghton Mifflin Co., 1997.

Broukal, Milada. *Idioms for Everyday Use.* National Textbook Co., 1993.

Collis, Harry. *101 American English Idioms: Understanding and Speaking English Like an American.* National Textbook Co., 1985.

Feare, Ronald E. *Everyday Idioms for Reference and Practice.* Addison-Wesley Publishing Co., 1997.

Makkai, Adam. *Dictionary of American Idioms.* Barrons Educational Series, 1995.

Pope, Lillie. *Word Play: Dictionary of Idioms.* Book Lab, 1998.

Spears, Richard A. *NTC's American Idioms Dictionary: The Most Practical Reference for the Everyday Expressions of Contemporary American English.* NTC Publishing Group, 2000.

Terban, Marvin. *Scholastic Dictionary of Idioms.* Scholastic, 1996.